Footsteps in Assisi

Footsteps in Assisi

Sara Lee Jobe

 PAULIST PRESS
NEW YORK AND MAHWAH, N.J.

All writings of St. Francis and St. Clare are from: *Francis and Clare, The Complete Works*, by R. Armstrong, OFM, and I. Brady, OFM. Copyright 1982 by the Missionary Society of St. Paul the Apostle in the State of New York. Reprinted by permission of Paulist Press.

The Song of the Sun of Francis of Assisi, translated by James Luguri as *The Song of the Sun*.

Cover and book design by James F. Brisson

Library of Congress Cataloging-in-Publication Data

Jobe, Sara Lee, 1931–
   Footsteps in Assisi / by Sara Lee Jobe.
     p.   cm.
  ISBN 0-8091-3635-X (alk. paper)
  1. Assisi (Italy) 2. Francis, of Assisi, Saint, 1182–1226—Homes and haunts. 3. Clare, of Assisi, Saint, 1194–1253—Homes and haunts. 4. Spiritual life—Christianity—History—Middle Ages, 600–1500. 5. Catholic Church—Doctrines—History. 6. Assisi (Italy)—Description. I. Title.
BX4700.F6J48 1996
271' .3—dc20
                                       96-3993
                                        CIP

Published by Paulist Press
997 Macarthur Boulevard
Mahwah, NJ 07430

Printed and bound in the
United States of America

This book is dedicated to

my friend,

Xavier J. Harris, O.F.M.

PREFACE

The pen and ink drawings in this book were made during two visits to Assisi—two weeks in 1988 and one week in 1993; both were in the month of May, a delightful time of year. During these periods I pursued my own quest for the spirit of Francis and Clare, a search that has changed my life. These sketches and writings are my reflections.

This book developed from a paper written for a course at the Franciscan School of Theology, Berkeley, California. The present work is the result of enthusiastic support and encouragement of many of my fellow students and teachers.

There are many I would like to acknowledge for both their encouragement and their constructive criticism. My particular appreciation goes to Fr. Xavier Harris, a true Franciscan, who has spiritually companioned me for many years on my journey. I would also like to thank Fleda Evans, my special friend, who constantly calls me to clarity of thought and word, and who has given me invaluable technical advice.

S.L.J.

Footsteps
in Assisi

"Pacz & Bene"

Where is the spirit of Francis to be found?
>The buildings, art, legends and holy places
>>become signs that call us to look
>>beyond;
>he is not likely to be found
>>in the remembrances presented
>>to the eye and the ear.
Look for him, instead,
>in the spirit and attitudes of the people—
>those which lead to
>>caring and love,
>>serving and concern,
>>prayer and humility;
>we find Francis in those who live in his spirit.

We also find Francis when we live in his spirit;
>then the white doves at the Carceri
>>might allow us to approach,
>and we may hear the rain and the butterfly
>>call out to us
>>to give praise and thanksgiving.
>We find him when we hear
>>the swallows and the larks
>>cry out our "Amen!"

We find Francis when we, too, discover
     the wealth offered in poverty
     and the freedom found in humility,
and when we, too, live
     with Christ as our brother
     and our brother as Christ.

When the act is transcended
     we meet the spirit of Francis;
when the attitude is transcended
     we meet the spirit of Christ.

Assisi
from Mt Subasio

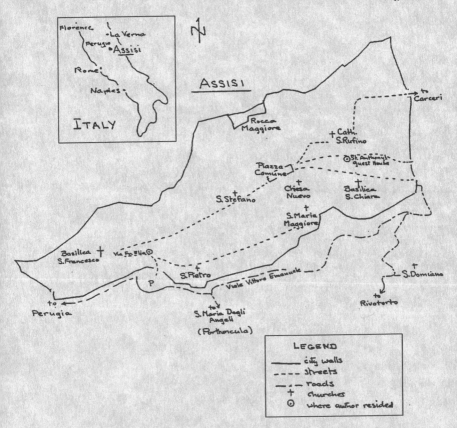

The walled city of Assisi is best viewed, perhaps, from the slopes of Mt. Subasio, below the Carceri. From here one sees the Umbrian Valley that lies at the foot of the city and cradles the precious Portiuncula within the Basilica of St. Mary of the Angels. Also prominent is the ruin of the Rocca Maggiore, a symbol of the political ordo of Francis' day. Below, standing above the trees and rooftops, are the churches, cathedrals and basilicas so important to the city's history. What might be found in the little walled city of Assisi?

3

Rocca Maggiore
Assisi

In Assisi
>the past
>is never too distant;
the ruin of the Rocca Maggiore,
>the place that offered
>sanctuary and protection,
still dominates this city
>that is so closely associated
>with Francis and Clare.

Rocca Maggiore

In Francis' youth
  the Rocca
 was brought to ruins,
    to be replaced by the walls
   that surround the city.
To whom does the villager,
  the merchant, the peasant,
 turn for protection?
    The Duke? The Pope? The Creator?

    Ghibellines or Guelphs,
   power does not bring peace.

THE LIFE OF FRANCIS

Francis was born in Assisi in 1182 to Pietro and Pica Bernardone. Pietro was a wealthy textile merchant. Although Francis was baptized Giovanni, Pietro gave him the nickname "Francesco." Having wealth and the *joie de vivre* of a troubadour, Francis became the spirited leader of Assisi's youth.

With the enthusiasm of a knight, Francis joined his fellow townsmen in an intercity skirmish with Perugia. In the first encounter Assisi was defeated and Francis was taken prisoner. He contracted a serious illness while in prison. After a year Francis, a changed young man, returned to Assisi to recuperate.

Francis then entered into an extended conversion experience. During this time he was inspired to care for lepers. In his Testament he wrote, "That which seemed bitter to me was changed into sweetness of soul and body." From this time on Francis ministered to the needs of the lepers.

Later, Francis responded to a call he received inspiring him to repair the chapel of San Damiano. He dramatically broke his affiliation with his family and chose to follow God's leading. In 1208, after hearing the missionary discourse from St. Matthew's Gospel, Francis committed himself to live the Gospel life. Filled with the love of Christ, he went among the common people as a mendicant preacher, proclaiming peace and living a life of penance. He took for his garb a rough tunic and rope belt. As *Il Poverello*, the Poor Little One, Francis lived humbly, working and begging, committed to *Madonna Poverta*, Lady Poverty.

Soon others were attracted by Francis' way of life. He later wrote, "The Lord gave me brothers." Francis and the brothers lived a life of Gospel simplicity. This way of life was to become the defining characteristic of the brotherhood.

Although Francis is best known as the Saint of Assisi, much of his life was spent on the way to or from hermitages, like the Carceri above Assisi, where he spent much time in prayer. Living closely with God and in personal union with Christ, Francis sought that "one thing necessary."

In 1223 Francis' Rule was approved by Pope Honorius III. In 1225, after receiving the stigmata, the marks of Jesus' passion, Francis composed the *Canticle of Brother Sun*. A year later, nearly blind and exhausted, he returned to the Portiuncula, where, surrounded by his brothers, he died on October 3, 1226. Recognized as a saint during his lifetime, he was officially canonized in 1228.

In the Middle Ages Assisi was a town
of divided loyalties and close-knit families
    whose homes had cribs filled
    with generations of children,
        the pride and hope of loving families.
Francis encouraged them
    to have their homes become
        the humble dwelling place of Jesus
        and the Holy Family.

In the town we find those elements
    so important to Francis' spirituality:
        the Crib, the Cross,
        and the Consecrated Presence.
    For Francis
        every dwelling had a Crib
            to welcome the infant Jesus,
        every poor and outcast person
            carried the Cross of Jesus,
        every church held the Consecrated
        Elements,
            the Real Presence of Christ.

Francis held a deep devotion to Mary.
    The womb of Mary embraced the Word of God;
    all creation became the manger that received him.

Hail, O Lady,

        holy Queen,

        Mary, holy Mother of God;

        you are the virgin made church

        and the one chosen

            by the most holy Father in heaven

        whom He consecrated

            with His most holy beloved Son

            and with the Holy Spirit the Paraclete,

        in whom there was and is

            all the fullness of grace and every good.

...And, Hail all you holy Virtues,

        which through the grace and light of the Holy Spirit

        are poured into the hearts of the faithful,

        so that from their faithless state

        you may make them faithful to God.

from *The Salutation of the Blessed Virgin*
St. Francis

All-powerful, most holy, most high and supreme God,

        holy and just Father,

        Lord, King of heaven and earth,

we thank You for Yourself

        for through Your holy will

        and through Your only Son

        with the Holy Spirit

        You have created all things spiritual and corporal

        and, having made us in Your own image and likeness,

        You placed us in paradise.

from *The Rule of 1221*
Chapter XXIII, Prayer and Thanksgiving
St. Francis

Today streets of Assisi
> are little changed,
> for within the change, the past remains—
>> the tile, the stone,
>> the stairs that become the arteries
>>> through which pedestrian traffic
>>> flows;
> the narrow streets
>> are better fit for horse, cart, and foot traffic
>> than today's cars and trucks.

Here the present moves
> within the framework of the past.
>> The Francis of history
>>> is held in Today;
>> the not-yet-known
>>> is soon to be encountered;
>> the almost forgotten
>>> is waiting to be remembered.

Assisi

As in a family portrait
    the old and the new stand together;
        ancient walls, still used,
        lean like tired patriarchs,
        flanked and upheld by more recent generations.
    They whisper the long-forgotten memories
        to occupant and visitor alike.
    The old and the young of the town
        are related—
        both buildings and people.

Houses overlooking
the Umbrian Valley

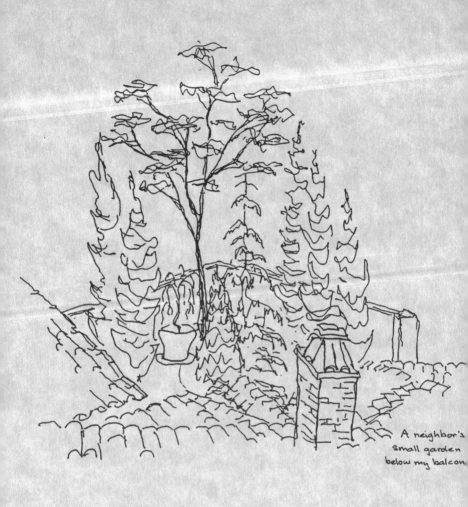

A neighbor's small garden below my balcon

Francis never tired
of his beloved
Assisi.

The same scene, seen repeatedly,
   if viewed without expectation,
   appears new and ever-changing.

There are aspects of Assisi
   that appear timeless:
         the placement of roof tiles,
         the walls of pink-tan limestone,
         the wrought-iron work,
   and the little gardens
         appreciated for their gifts.

from my window

One leaves the subdued light and coolness
     of the sanctuaries
to be greeted by the streets' charm,
     highlighted and shadowed by the sun.

From almost every street
one may look up
     to see flower pots
          on iron-work balconies
          and window ledges;
or one may look down
     upon roofs–
          textured, angular or curved,
     and walls
          that often contain tantalizing hints
          of the past.

Iron-work, stone buildings, cobbled streets
     and stair-step sidewalks
          pull the seeker of today
          into centuries past.

Chiesa Nuova

Sights in Assisi are never static or silent,

    for, accompanying all else,

    are the movements and sounds of the birds.

Dawn is heralded by their morning cries,

    as if beginning the day

    were their personal responsibility;

dusk is filled with the screeching

    of the evening feeding-frenzy

    as they momentarily swoop in formation,

    only to disperse in an instant

        at some bird-understood signal.

Everywhere, and at all times, there are the birds.

Across Fr Elias near Basilica

As both in the past
and in time to come,

  people rest upon windowsills
  and stand in doorways

    chatting with neighbors
    across the street
    or down the way—

      animated and comfortable
      as if sharing a cup of coffee.

  They still talk
    of that young man Francis,
    son of the cloth merchant.

Street
Market Assisi
near Piazza Comune

For several morning hours
      a street becomes a market.
Here there is
      an understandable pride in the produce
      and the quest for quality;
         both are honored
         by the seller and the buyer.

S. Rufino
from
St. Anthony's Guest House

Assisi has become a bridge

    that spans the chasm created by time,

    that separates the places called "past" and "present."

The element of time has little significance

    when one climbs the streets

        where Francis joyfully greeted his neighbors,

        or spends time in a chapel

            he lovingly repaired,

        or walks quietly in the garden

            where Clare so often prayed.

Awe and wonder

    move with their own accord, unbidden,

    pulling the seeker into the presence of the saints.

When Assisi is met with an open spirit
      we are joined in an intimate way
            with Francis and Clare.
They no longer lived long ago;
      we are unexpectedly reminded
of their nearness
      when walking where they have walked,
      or sitting silently where they have prayed,
      or realizing this is a place they knew so well.

Francis and Clare are near, in Assisi,
      among both the townspeople
      and the Franciscans,
         living with those who seek them today.

How intense is the spirit
      instilled by Francis and Clare!
         When touched by it,
         one is impelled to follow.

Francis lived life in the Kingdom of God.
　　With Christ-like love he ministered to others;
　　　　they were his beloved,
　　　　　for they were Christ's loved ones.
Francis' love for Christ
　　and his awareness of Christ's presence
　　in all creation
　　　　became his *raison d'être*.

Umbria became the earthly cathedral
where Francis walked with God—
  the rocky mountains were
    its walls built of stone,
  the rich valleys and refreshing streams
    its sanctuary floor
    and baptismal font,
  the sky and clouds, sun, moon and stars
    its heavenly windows and altar candles.
 Both the rich and the wretched
    formed its worshiping congregation,
    bound as one in God's love
    through the cross of Christ.

In this cathedral
  Francis, the "Idiota of Assisi,"
    sang and preached,
    worked and prayed,
    worshiped and loved his God.
      Yet, in this simple, complex man
      the people saw a saint,
        the presence of Christ.

Holy Poverty destroys

> the desire of riches

> and avarice

> and the cares of this world.

Holy Humility destroys

> pride

> and all the people who are in the world

> and all things that belong to the world.

Holy Charity destroys

> every temptation of the devil and of the flesh

> and every carnal fear.

Holy Obedience destroys

> every wish of the body and of the flesh

> and binds its mortified body

>> to obedience of the Spirit

>> and to obedience of one's brother;

> and [that person] is subject and submissive

>> to all persons in the world

>> and not to man only

>> but even to all beasts and wild animals,

> so that they may do whatever they want with him

> inasmuch as it has been given to them from above

>> by the Lord.

from *The Salutation of the Virtues*
St. Francis

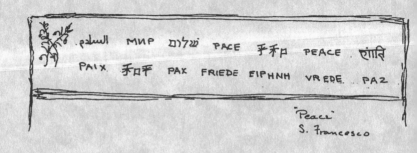

السلام MИP שלום PACE 平和 PEACE शांति
PAIX 和平 PAX FRIEDE EIPHNH VREDE PAZ

"Peace"
S. Francesco

Not to be overlooked
was Francis' gentle love for Mary,
the mother of Christ,
and her intimate relationship
to all that is in the Kingdom,
to all that contains God's presence.

The way was open for his special relationship
to Clare and her Poor Ladies
as their community embraced Francis' unique
spirituality,
its richness found in a life lived
in poverty and humility.

THE LIFE OF CLARE

Clare was born in 1194 into one of Assisi's noble families, the Favorones, supporters of the Ghibellines. In 1210 she heard Francis preach in the Cathedral of San Rufino, where they had both been baptized, and chose to follow his way of living the Gospel life. On the night of Palm Sunday, 1212, she secretly left her home and joined Francis and his followers at the Portiuncula. There Clare was shorn of her hair, given a simple tunic and cord, and put under the protection of the Church. Francis and the brothers secreted her away to a Benedictine monastery where she was soon joined by her sister, Agnes, much to the displeasure of her family. She would later be joined by Ortolana, her mother.

Later that year she and Agnes began to reside at San Damiano. They were soon joined by others and were known as the "Poor Ladies of San Damiano." There Clare, who referred to herself as the "little plant" of Francis, and her "little flowers" lived a life humbly dedicated to prayer, labor, and poverty. They lived as an enclosed, contemplative community, the only option available to women religious at the time. Clare rejected any fixed income or the ownership of properties as means of support, the accepted practice for religious communities in the Middle Ages. The community's physical needs were met by their own labors and the town's generosity; their spiritual needs were ministered to by Francis and the brothers.

Clare knew herself to have a close relationship to the Mystical Body of Christ, and she was gifted with great spiritual insights. Her strong faith led her, alone, to confront and intimidate a band of Saracens. Although obviously a dynamic leader, she did not desire a position of authority within her community. Clare was very demanding of herself, and as a result greatly compromised her own health. She was confined to bed for the last twenty-five years of her life.

Clare closely followed Francis' Rule. A woman of gentle spirit, deep love and great purposefulness, she had, perhaps, as profound an influence on Francis as he had on her. One cannot but think that her close adherence to Francis' way of life encouraged him to hold to those standards he desired for his own rather fractious brothers. Because she insisted upon the "privilege of poverty" as a part of the Rule, popes were unwilling to grant an approval for such an austere form of life for women. In 1253, two days before her death, her Rule was approved. This Order is know as the Second Order of St. Francis, the Poor Clares. Clare was canonized two years after her death.

If you suffer with Him, you shall reign with Him;
>> if you weep with Him, you shall rejoice with Him;
>> if you die with Him on the cross of tribulation,
>>> you shall possess heavenly mansions
>>> in the splendor of the saints,
>>> and in the Blood of Life, your name shall be called
>>>> glorious among men.

from *The Third Letter*
to Blessed Agnes of Prague
St. Clare

Place your mind
>> before the mirror of eternity.

Place your soul
>> in the brilliance of glory.

Place your heart
>> in the figure of the divine substance.

and transform your whole being
into the Image of the Godhead Itself
>> through contemplation.

from *The Third Letter*
to Blessed Agnes of Prague
St. Clare

Living in austerity
>Clare found herself rich
>>in the most desired element: Poverty.
>Clare cherished her silence
>>within the cloister walls—
>>>heart, opened in prayer,
>>>hands, busied with work,
>>>spirit, at rest in God.
>She found herself freed
>>from earthly demands;
>>>she knew herself to be touching
>>>the heart of God.
Clare embodied the spirit
of Lady Poverty.

In the Lord Jesus Christ, I admonish and
exhort all my sisters, both those present and
those to come, to strive always to imitate the way
of holy simplicity, humility, and poverty, and [to
preserve] the integrity of [our] holy manner of life,
as we were taught by our blessed Father Francis
from the beginning of our conversion to Christ.
Thus may they always remain in the fragrance of
a good name, both among those who are far off
and those who are near. [This will take place] not
by our own merits but solely by the mercy and
grace of our Benefactor, the Father of mercies.

from *The Testament of Saint Clare*

Never regretting the life she left,
        Clare, compromised in health
        and courageous in spirit,
                walked in spiritual companionship
                with Francis.
        They were a spiritually united family,
                the Lesser Brothers
                and the Poor Ladies.

        Embracing poverty,
        dedicated to prayer,
        owning nothing,
                Clare, the "Little Plant" of Francis,
                and the sisters, the "Little Flowers" of Clare,
                        were clothed with radiance,
                        crowned with a bride's diadem.

        They were
        the spiritual bouquet of Assisi.

Since by divine inspiration you have made yourselves daughters and servants of the most high King, the heavenly Father, and have taken the Holy Spirit as your spouse, choosing to live according to the perfection of the holy Gospel, I resolve to promise for myself and for my brothers always to have the same loving care and special solicitude for you as [I have] for them.

The Form of Life Given to Saint Clare and Her Sisters by St. Francis

San Damiano

"...whoever gives a cup of cold water to one
of these lowly ones...will not want for his reward."

Matthew 10:42

The garden of San Damiano
    is infused with
    an air of calm,
    the scent of roses,
    and the spirit of Clare.
In the serenity
    an unrealized thirst
    is quenched;
        the spirit comes to the well.

Today, those who follow Francis and Clare
    live close to the charism of their leaders;
    they do not direct their footsteps toward the past.
Rather, the past walks with them;
    the spirits of Francis and Clare are historically present.
The Franciscan spirit does not seek to imitate the past,
    but those who live in it
    seek to be the present expression of God's love
        to the world around them,
            to live in simple, humble service,
            prayer and love.

Franciscans bring a faith-filled simplicity
    and uncompromising ethic,
        calling a people
        to be true to their Vision
            and a church
            to be true to its foundations.

As a knight might court a damsel,
    Francis pursued Lady Poverty;
        many do not wish to honor
        or recognize her gifts.
With the soul of a poet
    and the ways of a beggar,
        Francis lived with the riches offered
        by his brother, the King.

Poverty has little to do with material possessions; it is an attitude toward possessing and desir-
ing those elements which separate one from others
and from God. One enters into this much as one
would choose to enter a room. It becomes a
"space," a space that encompasses a personal
truth. It is both free and unbounded; it is not to be
considered devoid or lacking, but is to be valued for
the freedom it offers—a space into which something
or someone may enter, perhaps to remain or to stay
but for a moment, then freely leave. Because this
unlimited space is not filled with expectations or
desires, it is hospitable to all. Whatever or whoever
comes into this environment is received as Gift, and if
nothing enters, that becomes Gift, too.

Francis chose to live in this space of poverty. This
is not entered into lightly or too quickly, for it necessi-
tates a certain degree of maturity to desire the humility
to possess nothing; this includes expectations, desires,
security, importance and other self-limiting attitudes.
The identity of "self" must be developed sufficiently in
order that one may voluntarily deny it. Francis so closely identified with Christ that he became freed of his lim-
iting identity as Francis Bernardone.

Much as a cloak protects against the cold, a deep
spiritual life gave Francis an inner strength and forti-
tude, making it possible for him to endure physical
hardships, suffering and rigorous asceticism. Living the
Gospel life, Francis, the Poverello, could walk with
Christ-like freedom in poverty and humility.

Hail, Queen Wisdom, may the Lord protect you
    with your sister, holy pure Simplicity.
Lady, holy Poverty, may the Lord protect you
    with your sister, holy Humility.
Lady, holy Charity, may the Lord protect you
    with your sister, holy Obedience.
O most holy Virtues, may the Lord protect all of you,
    from whom you come and proceed.
There is surely no one in the entire world
    who can possess any one of you
    unless he dies first.
Whoever possesses any one [of you]
    and does not offend the others,
    possesses all.
And whoever offends one [of you]
    does not possess any
    and offends all.

from *The Salutation of the Virtues*
St. Francis

In his mysticism Francis found meaning in all he had seen and experienced. His time spent in prayer, usually in hermitages, led him to deep spiritual insights. There he found the sacredness of reality. St. John's words, "Through Him all things came into being, and apart from Him nothing came to be," became life to Francis—all the varied images of the present Christ.

Seeking a life of humility and poverty, Francis sought to be emptied of his self-restricting values. Only then could everything be accepted as Gift, thereby freely allowing the Gift to be transformed into the wealth that is God. The illusion of possession does not allow this to happen. Francis experienced the created, transcended the created, and was transformed by the created. Even the sought-for poverty was created by God; only in humility could it be accepted, for in humility it was formed and offered. Through the mystical experience in prayer Francis could join with God in seeking true, complete simplicity.

Francis sought to respond to God's love
by living as Jesus did
in every facet of his life;
for him the only way to Christ
was through the Cross.
Toward the end of his life,
broken in body and spirit,
he prayed on Mt. Alverna
for the loving obedience of Jesus.
How closely he identified with Jesus
was reflected in his receiving
the wounds of Christ.
He now lived with the marks of the Cross.

...Write that I bless all my brothers, [those] who are in the Order, and [those] who will come until the end of the world.....I make known my will to my brothers briefly in these three phrases, namely, as a sign that they remember my blessing and my testament:

let them always love one another,
let them always love and be faithful
to our Lady Holy Poverty,
and let them always be faithful and subject
to the prelates and all clerics
of Holy Mother Church.

from *The Testament Written in Siena*
St. Francis

...And after the Lord gave me some brothers, there
was nobody to show me what to do; but the Most High
himself revealed to me that I was to live according
to the form of the Holy Gospel. And I caused
it to be written down simply and in a few words,
and the Lord Pope approved it for me. And those
who came to take up this life gave all they could
possess to the poor, and they were content with one
tunic patched inside and out if they wished, besides
a cincture and drawers. And we wished to have
nothing else.

from The Testament of St. Francis

S. Stefano

It is said
that the bell of San Stefano tolled
    at the hour of Francis' death;
        an historic or mythic truth
        it matters not.

San Stefano

This Romanesque church
is deceptive in its plainness,
        its stone sanctuary and apse unadorned
        except for two narrow windows
            strangely offset
            behind the altar.
This church is a holy place,
    so rich in simplicity
    it seemingly has little to offer.
        Casual tourists stay only a moment;
        those who remain
            become reverently quiet.
No one even whispers in San Stefano;
        the worshiper is pulled into the depth
        of this silence.

Here one may sit in prayer for unmeasured time
    on the narrow, rigid, wooden benches,
    seemingly alone and waiting—
        only to discover the spirit of Francis
        is already there.

Santa Maria Maggiore

Francis loved the Faith.

      Every church was cherished

      and to be kept immaculate

            for it was a tabernacle

            that held the Consecrated Presence of Christ.

      Upon entering a church he would say,

            "We adore You, Lord Jesus Christ,

            here and in all Your churches in the world;

            and we bless You,

            for through Your holy cross

            You have redeemed the world."

S. Francesco

In the Chapel of the Blessed Sacrament,
    before the consecrating altar,
    who is not humbled by God's gift of Self,
        to be received
        in the body and blood of Christ?

How uncomfortable Francis might have been
in this, his house of worship!
    Missing, or concealed by the aura of grandness,
    is the richness of poverty
    and the strength of humility.
        Where is Francis' vision
        of best serving God
        by serving the least among us?

Let the whole of mankind tremble,

the whole world shake

and the heavens exult

when Christ, the Son of the living God,

is present on the altar

in the hands of the priest.

O admirable heights and sublime lowliness!

O sublime humility!

O humble sublimity!

That the Lord of the universe,

God and the Son of God,

so humbles Himself

that for our salvation

He hides Himself under the little form of bread!

Look, brothers, at the humility of God

and pour out your hearts before Him!

Humble yourselves, as well,

that you may be exalted by Him.

Therefore,

hold back nothing of yourselves for yourselves

so that

He Who gives Himself totally to you

may receive you totally.

from *A Letter to the Entire Order*
St. Francis

Neighbors to S. Chiara

Santa Chiara, creating depth,
both dominates the scene
and becomes an unconscious backdrop.

Santa Chiara
Assisi

The churches, like Francis and Clare,
    hold a predominant position
    in the lives of the people;
        they are both a setting
            for religious expression
      and a background
            against which life is lived.

Francis responded
both spiritually and physically
    to the words he heard,
        "Francis, go repair my church which,
        as you see, is falling completely into ruin."
He heeded the words of Scripture:
    "Humbly welcome the word that has been planted
    in you and is able to save your souls."
                    James 1:21

Francis accepted the grace offered
    to claim his true identity:
        an obedient child of God,
        a humble servant to the disenfranchised,
        and Christ's brother among brothers.
    In this he found the meaning of life.

S. Damiano

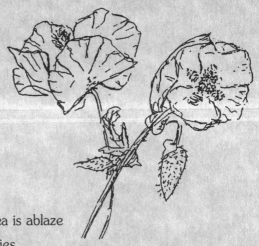

In May the area is ablaze
with red poppies
       on the hillsides, under the olive trees,
       and scattered throughout the cultivated fields
          bordered by tall, fresh-leafed trees.
These delicate flowers are
       the color of change
          from winter to spring,
          from death to life,
          from crucifixion to resurrection;
       they are the color of hope,
          of promise, of waiting,
          of God's presence in re-creation.

Red'—
       the color of blood, the color of life,
       the color of Francis' love
       of the crucified Jesus.

S. Damiano

The road to San Damiano
        invites the traveler
        into the intimacy of touching its history—
                like that which one experienced
                when holding grandfather's walking-stick
                or opening the family Bible
                        carefully penned with ancestors'
                        names and dates.

This humble church holds
        both the comfort of the familiar
        and an awe of the unknown.

S. Maria del Angeli
from S. Damiano

In his quest to follow Jesus
    Francis sought the company of Lady Poverty
    to companion him through life.

It seems appropriate
        that the church in which Francis responded
        to God's call
                became, at an early date,
                the center for women's spirituality,
                a place of refuge
                for Clare and her Poor Ladies.

Looking toward the Portiuncula from San Damiano,
        this view undoubtedly strengthened
        and maintained
                the spiritual well-being
                of Clare and her "little flowers."

Clare was among those in Assisi
    who heard Francis' message
    and responded in heart and spirit;
        she chose the peace-filled way,
        saying "Yes" to a life
            of poverty, work and prayer.

The light radiating from Clare
    was not dimmed by cloister walls;
        it shone upon the countryside
        and far across the continent.
    Others desired to follow
    her gentle way of life.

Francis learned much from Clare
    and was guided by her insight and actions;
    some say he learned from her
        to minister to the poor
        and care for the lepers.

San Damiano
Assisi.

The sanctuary of San Damiano
is where Clare and her Ladies worshiped.
    This small and sacred space
        which Francis re-built,
        and which, in turn, re-formed the man,
    embraces the intimate relationship between
        the call and the response,
        the spiritual and the physical,
        the stone-setter and the stone,
        the animate and the inanimate.
    To the ceiling and walls
        clings the softening effect
        of thousands of candle-hours—
            the presence of prayer
            made evident.

glimpses of
S. Damiano

Living the Gospel life,
Francis, Clare, and their followers
    were free
    to respond to God.
There were no possessions
    that demanded concern
    or desires to be filled;
they had nothing, yet had everything.
    This way of life is only difficult
    in its simplicity.
With Christ, both Francis and Clare would live
    the joy-filled, pain-filled experience
    of sacrificial love;
        they would also know
        a dimension of eternal life.

What you hold, may you always hold.

What you do, may you always do and never abandon.

But with swift pace, light step,

    and unswerving feet,

    so that even your steps stir up no dust,

go forward

    securely, joyfully, and swiftly,

on the path of prudent happiness,

    believing nothing which would dissuade you

     from this resolution

    or which would place a stumbling block

    for you on the way....

from *The Second Letter*
to *Blessed Agnes of Prague*
St. Clare

San Damiano

San Damiano presents a collage
of the many ways the brothers
continue the presence of Francis;
various details point to
the importance of
silence, prayer,
and the sacredness of Mary,
the importance of
humility and simplicity,
hospitality and privacy.

Walls declare
the boundaries of S. Damiano

A storm from the Umbrian Valley

whips cypress trees

      into a ballet of spiraling motion—

          eternal flames

          carrying the spirit ever upward.

On a farmhouse near Rivotorto
fieldstones enable roof tiles
to resist the elements,
much as faith has become
the foundation of the family—
old ways
become tradition.

Brother Leo, [wish] your Brother Francis health and peace!

I speak to you, my son, as a mother. I place all the words which we spoke on the road in this phrase, briefly and [as] advice. And afterwards, if it is necessary for you to come to me for counsel, I say this to you: In whatever way it seems best to you to please the Lord God and to follow in His footprints and His poverty, do this with the blessing of God and my obedience. And if you believe it necessary for the well-being of your soul, or to find comfort, and you wish to come to me, Leo, come!

A Letter to Brother Leo
St. Francis

Listen, little poor ones called by the Lord,

who have come together from many parts and provinces:

Live always in truth,

that you may die in obedience.

Do not look at the life outside,

for that of the Spirit is better.

I beg you through great love,

to use with discretion

the alms which the Lord gives you.

Those who are weighed down by sickness

and the others who are wearied because of them,

all of you: bear it in peace.

For you will sell this fatigue at a very high price

and each one [of you] will be crowned queen

in heaven with the Virgin Mary.

The Canticle of Exhortation
to Saint Clare and Her Sisters
St. Francis

Francis and Clare gave to others
> the only thing they would call their own:
> God's love;
>> and so, in this way,
>> they had immeasurable wealth.

St. Francis' Olive
Eremo Carceri

Immediately outside the cave used by Francis as a chapel, the mountain drops off sharply; a stream far below is barely heard. A step-path leads along the outside of the Carceri to a place where the water pools, then cascades over a resistant ledge, deepening its channel below. Near the bridge that spans the narrow gorge is an old olive tree, said to have been growing there in Francis' time.

Outside the chapel
     between the cool of the cave
     and the warmth of the sun,
          time remains suspended;
     white doves fan the air in silent sounds.
Here it is possible to be among others
     yet remain alone,
     in moments of anytime—
          a time for reflection and prayer,
          a time to be with Francis.

This dark and cool cave
      was a place of aloneness,
      the womb of re-creation.

The changing man would emerge
      from his place of prayer
      a committed person.
It was here
      the illusive became a reality;
      he would no longer live apart from God.

Almighty God,

and You my Lord Jesus Christ,

I pray You

> to enlighten me

> and to dispel the darkness of my spirit;

give me

> a faith that is without limit,

> a hope that is ever unfailing,

> and a love that is universal.

Grant, O my God,

> that I may really know You

> and that I may be guided in all things

>> according to Your light

>> and in conformity with Your will.

A Prayer of St. Francis

Mt. Subasio's
Creatures

"In him everything on heaven and on earth
was created, things visible and invisible."

Colossians 1:16

Francis embraced all creation
as the glory of God;
    all that was created
    celebrated both the created and the Creator.
There was an inter-connectedness between
being praise and giving praise;
    for Francis everything in creation
    declared the glory of God.
    "My God and my All," he would say.

72

Canticle of Brother Sun

Exalted, most able, and good Lord,

Yours are all praises and glory, honor and every blessing.

  Their source is only in you.

Not a one of us is worthy to take you on our lips.

Be praised then, my Lord, in company with all your creation,

Most especially our great brother the sun;

  He brings us the day filling the world with light,

  Beautiful and beaming, his resplendence

Arouses us to imagine your face.

Be praised, my Lord, through our sister the moon

    and the many stars;

  You shaped them in brightness,

    made them beloved and lovely.

My Lord, be praised through our brother wind

  And through the sky, cloudy then

    clearing, creating the seasons

  Through whose turnings you continue creation.

Be praised, my Lord, through our sister water,

  So helpful and so unpretentious, precious and simple.

My Lord, be praised through our brother flame;

  Through him your radiance reaches into the night;

  He is handsome and merry, eager and strong.

And, my Lord, be praised through earth our sister and mother;
        She feeds us and shapes us, for us
She gives birth to fruit of all kinds,
            Flowers of every color, grains and grasses.

Be praised, my Lord, through all people who learn in your love
                to pardon each other,
        Who endure in their weakness,
                are not undone as they suffer.
        They come to know joy becoming grounded in peace;
You are yourself, O God, their great reward.

My Lord, be praised at last through our sister death;
        Nothing living can prevent her visit.
        Only they are lost who have already died in their sin.
Happy are those whom dying discovers alive with the life
                you have willed us to live;
        No deeper death can do them harm.

Let all creation praise, consent and be grateful;
Let us take our place in the humbleness of being who we are.

St. Francis
(translated as *Song of the Sun*
by James Luguri)

Certainly the earth
      had been touched by heaven,
      for had it not received
            the first Eucharist,
            the Body of Christ?
      And had it not witnessed
            the Easter Event,
            the Paschal Mystery of New Life?

Alone, in the quiet,
 the desires of Self
  may be silenced;
 then the Word may be formed
  and its divine fullness received.
Poverty is filled with creative activity—
 only in that space
 may Desire be transformed,
  to be received and held
  as Gift.
 Here Death is no longer a loss.

All-powerful, most holy,

most high, and supreme God:

all good,

totally good,

You Who alone are good

may we give You

all praise, all glory,

all thanks, all honor,

all blessing,

and all good things.

So be it.

So be it.

Amen.

from *The Praises To Be Said at All the Hours*
St. Francis

"God has given us the wisdom
to understand fully the mystery."

Ephesians 1:10

Sitting quietly on the slopes of Mt. Subasio,
   overlooking the city,
   the individuality of creation
   claims its sacredness;
      one becomes a part of
      the Canticle of Brother Sun:
         "Most high, all-powerful, all good Lord!
         All praise is yours, all glory, all honor
         And all blessing."

Where is the spirit of Francis?

Where is Francis to be found?   In the town
    the streets bustle with the activity of tourists.
        Foreign words are interspersed
        with the familiar: "Francesco," "Chiara," "Dio";
    and the townspeople, living the dailiness of life,
        exuberantly accent themselves
        with either full or muted voices
        accompanied by waving hands.
  And everyone mindfully considers the traffic—
        cars race in reverse down a one-way street;
        trucks, seemingly oblivious to pedestrians,
        hurl their imposing presence
           down the narrow streets.

Where is Francis?   Along the street
    there is an open market;
        the sounds of commerce
        intermingle with the smells of sweet fruit
        and vegetables still touched with damp earth.

In a semi-dark half-basement
          a metal worker labors,
                    the air pungent with the acrid odor
                    of hot iron, oil and welding;
another basement,
          covered with sawdust and wood chips,
          pulses with the sounds of saw and rasp.

Where is Francis?   In the churches
          small groups speculate
                    about the hidden secrets—now obliterated,
                    torn down, built over, or remodeled—
                              to be reconstructed in the imagination.
          Groups vibrate
                    with enthusiasm
                    or remain silent, in awe,
                              having been touched by The Mystery.

Where is Francis?
          The spirit of Francis may be found
                    here,   in Assisi.

"Pace e Bene"

"Take nothing for the journey"
then,
everything received
comes
as Gift.

Glossary

Basilica   Named after an oblong Roman building, ending in a semicircular apse, used for court and public assembly. The term was then used to refer to a style of building. The early Christian basilicas had naves, clerestoried aisles, and high transepts. It presently refers to a Roman Catholic church given ceremonial privileges.

Carceri   A hermitage comprised of numerous caves on the slopes of Mt. Subasio where Francis and many of the brothers spent extended time in prayer. The present extensive building encompasses several of the caves. Lovely paths lead to other caves.

Cathedral   The home church of the bishop of a diocese; the chair (cathedra) of the bishop is located here.

Chapel   A small building, or separate part of a larger church, used for worship.

Church   The building in which the people come together for worship. The assembled people are also referred to as the Church.

Clare   St. Clare, an early follower of Francis. See Biography. Italian: *Chiara*.

Consecrated Elements   The bread and wine that contains the Real Presence of Christ.

Francis   St. Francis of Assisi. See Biography.

Ghibelline   The aristocratic political party supporting the authority of the German emperors in medieval Italy.

Guelph   The papal and popular political party that opposed the authority of the German emperors in medieval Italy.

Kingdom of God   Life in accordance with God's divine plan.

Order   A group of people living under a particular rule, having taken a vow to abide by the directives of that group.

Ordo   The accepted divisions and behaviors that established the order of a classed society.

Poor Ladies   Clare and her followers; during Clare's time, those who lived at San Damiano.

Portiuncula   The "Little Portion," a small chapel dedicated to St. Mary of the Angels, repaired by Francis, where the Franciscan movement began; it was around this chapel that he and his early followers lived. It is now enclosed within the Basilica of St. Mary of the Angels (Basilica di S. Maria Degli Angeli).

Poverello   "The Poor Little One," a term Francis used in referring to himself.

Rocca Maggiore   Originally built as a Roman garrison, in 1174 became the fortress of the feudal nobility. It was partially destroyed in Francis' youth (1198) by the people of the commune and later rebuilt.

Rule   An order of life, including its vision and purpose, restrictions and regulations, that has been approved by the Church. Francis' Rule was approved in 1223, Clare's in 1253.

Saracens   Marauding unbelievers.

Tabernacle   A receptacle for the reserved sacrament. It is placed on a stand or in a wall niche.